www.finishinglinepress.com

Theory Headed Dragon

poems by

Carol Dorf

Finishing Line Press
Georgetown, Kentucky

Theory Headed Dragon

ACKNOWLEDGMENTS

"The Persistence of Objects" *Sin Fronteras*, Spring 2015
"In The Anti-Room," "All That Remains," *Tidal Basin Review*, 2015
"Early Morning Train," *Poetry Superhighway*, May 2014
"Finding Myself Strange" *Poemeleon*, February 2014
"On Definitions," *Antiphon*, Issue Three, 2012, reprinted in *Scientific
American* online, Fall 2013
"The Truth is Mending," *27 rue de fleures*, fall 2012, reprinted in *What
Matters Anthology*, Jacar Press, Summer 2014
"Weather Forecast" *Hot Metal Bridge*, Fall 2013
"Nude Suite," *The Mom Egg*, 2013
"On the Way Out of the Memory Palace," *Talking Writing*, March 2013
"Announce the Hour," *Maintenant 7*, 2013
"Prescription 1," *Antiphon*, Issue 5, Autumn 2012
"The Thing Itself," *27 rue de fleures*, 2012
"Gravity," *Beltway*, Summer 2012
"On Definitions," *Antiphon* Issue Three, 2012
"Lace," *Qarrtsiluni*, 2012
"The Theory Headed Dragon," *The Midway*, 2007

Editor: Christen Kincaid

Cover Art: Terri Saul

Author Photo: Carol Dorf

Cover Design: Josh Michels

Printed in the USA on acid-free paper.
Order online: www.finishinglinepress.com
also available on amazon.com

Author inquiries and mail orders:
Finishing Line Press
P. O. Box 1626
Georgetown, Kentucky 40324
U. S. A.

Table of Contents

For Rebecca, who has brought so much conversation into my life.

"The trap is the use of the discoveries of science instead of the methods of science."

Muriel Rukeyser, from *The Life of Poetry*

Why Are You Always Writing Elegies?

At first light you want to recall
the dawn chorus of your childhood
and compare it to sound's
relative scarcity; though not all
sounds are scarce around here:
sirens, trains, people talking
as they rush to the station, music
blasting out of souped-up cars.

Be honest though, if any place
still has much of a dawn chorus outside
of an official park it could well be here,
what with organic mamas growing
sunflowers and beans in mulched
back yards, and flowers in patterns
approaching a meadow for the butterflies,
and gardens where people say,
"I just don't have the time, let's see what volunteers."

The other day, on your way
into the DMV, a hummingbird swooped
past. Though who can tell if this
says much about the dawn chorus—
consumed by feral cats, and the little bit
of Roundup someone can't resist
when it's time to sell a house—
so what is your share of the blame?

Late to the Party

In the US of A even the homeless
clutch cell phones, pay-as-you-go offering
temporary citizenship; the way
fleabag hotels offered temporary residence
to men like my father who had trouble
keeping track of themselves.

Pocket gadgets allow the generous State
to track every call, every search for
shoes or fertilizer, all the cafes you frequent,
for minimal monthly payments.

Verisimilitude fells Center City,
where my father paced Locust, Walnut,
Spruce, Pine, Lombard, South,
where shopping mall facades
promise cases of the new, all
with handy chips to prevent loss.

Consider the State (or the City)
redeveloping every last residential hotel
into architecturally significant offices,
and penthouse apartment buildings.

Thank God, my father's long gone—
were he still around, maybe
some shiny social worker would offer him
a spot in a transitional house—
exactly what transition left unspecified.

But who's not in favor of this party?
Webbed together in constant conversation,
we exchange location snaps while
the self-help site for schizophrenics
advises carrying a cell phone
when talking to your voices.

You know, even a paranoid
from Sigmund Freud like my father,
famous for the attempt to teach
his son to fly off a hotel roof,
can be right once or twice a day.

Weather Forecast

Who can manage without a life jacket
zipped tight across the chest, arms like wings,
white and gray as a gull, though you might long
for the parrot's or the peacock's acquaintance

with color. Even the pigeon screams iridescent
pleasure when the laboratory doors open
and she flies to the crenellated roof—
a noun calling "hope," or "glove,"

or "fireworks," which actually birds detest;
the way a small child cowers in the car
when everyone else climbs the hill to catch
intersecting explosions of color.

After the fireworks, what comes next—
questions reorder history until there is nothing
to eat but bills; reports warn of more
explosions; thunder pursues our air-

conditioned visions—small increments of heat.
Who wants to be the parent nagging children
to turn off the lights, or an annoying child
patrolling the house with a wrench to cure leaks.

In the surprise of the new century, parrots
are moving north, adaptable and hungry.

Lace

Nothing is what they say when
they've gone past wish into blankness,
white hole of open time

Our suggestions cluster
overblown chrysanthemums
weighing down their stems

This antidote to desire
to the white field that empties
into a single point

Until context disappears,
overwashed fibers laid out to dry
on brown summer grasses

Each flower's center questions
color, the way in the small
world of moles light is texture

Before speech, inquisitive
babble, a small hand pointing
to the unidentified

When the world held wild and remote,
when the edges of the fields remained
uncultivated for the small creatures

How resilient a gesture

Fungible

He said, agreeing with his father,
that jobs should move like a yoga master
stretching through sun salutation,
then catching a plane to another country.
Outsource is nothing like the locavore bistro
in search of the freshest ingredients.

Outsource is the fungible who wait
outside the supermarket, hands
outstretched; but this market is far
from the one where he shops, far
from a location where private security
patrols comfortable illusions.

The Thing Itself

Physicists declare new knowledge
of reality: particles that may
(or may not) be travelling
faster than the speed of light.

The colossal sun expands as it cools,
but that time is further away
than the congealing of dust
into planets, so don't worry so much.
November rains have striped away
the last red persimmon leaves.
This happens every year—perceived
climate fluctuations are not the same thing
as evidence of long-term change.

On the plus side, one could say
our weather grows more exciting—
less storm chasing, and more experience
of disaster arriving on the doorstep
suitcase in hand, asking to bunk on the sofa
for a week, a month, the long term.
If the vast changes in the atmosphere
continue, we might want to add some
rooms to the house for the displaced.

Announce the Hour You Have Clocks For

Time progresses through the bells
announcing each moment of occupation:
toilet, wash, dress, eat, work a, break, work b . . .
eat, undress, wash, toilet.

Schematic, yes. Our clocks' precision
increases until the second,
the thousandth's of a second
separates competitors for the title,
"Fastest Woman in the World,"
"Fastest Man."

Could Mussolini have made these trains
run on fractional time? For a space-
ship it matters, a millisecond off
and three years later Mars will be far
from its predicted location.

Yet who doesn't long for the time
of a mother soothing a fretful child to sleep.
"It's the middle of the night, hush, rest."

In the Anti-Room

The Anti-Room fills with the No's
of a campaign year, like leftover posters
that never make it into the recycling bin.
Small children tantrum in the center
of the floor, and adults assiduously
ignore them. Some of the furniture appears
comfortable, but when you sit in the easy chair,
you sink until your knees rise to chest level.
The music in the background alternates
between torch singers, kill-the-machine punk,
cop-fight rap, and old news, stuck in a shuffle
over which no one exerts any control. The coffee
is cold, and the cookies have been arrayed in open
trays for days. Even the teenagers refuse them,
demanding money to go to the corner store
after dark. Eventually the children slide
into uneasy sleep, startling awake at the sound
of each backfiring truck. The people who had plans
for fixing up this space have long since left
to revitalize other neighborhoods,
developing new varieties of urban bees.

The Persistence of Objects

Dying stars throw out diamond dust,
mark a trail of what once was;
the way we leave behind houses full
of objects that must be hauled off
to imagined reuse at Goodwill, bags
of papers and reusable containers
for the dump and permanence
sealed beneath the earth.

And then you turn on the computer
see image after image of what someone else
has left behind: grandfather clocks,
and mantle clocks paired with candlesticks,
clocks with keys, clocks with pendulums
all to count the analog world.
How did my grandparents clock
with flipping numbers arrive
in this category: Clocks, antique?

Our quantum brains process
fragments we see between blinks
as continuous. Even touch susceptible
to neuron fatigue, flickering electrical
impulses. Why are you sitting in the dark?
Like Alice when you pick up a book,
it says "Read Me," promises changes,
conversation between the queen
and a suited mole, while in a quite unlikely
physics, your clothes still fit.

You accept suspension of disbelief
until argument disperses the axioms
that had been so comforting along
with the disintegrating blanket,
and girlhood's little diary
hidden beneath the mattress.

Early Morning Train

Did I tell you that whenever I see a train
in a European landscape, I feel nervous. Well
maybe not a commuter train, but one
of those large engines with smoke rising

above the tracks, and those brick buildings
in the background, fences alongside the track.
This summer, going from Enschede to Berlin, alone
on the train. Well, it was a commuter train

with plenty of windows to watch the landscape.
So much water. Those games we played,
when I was a child, a long time ago.
Almost all of those Nazis are dead

though there's always something else,
like Skinheads and new Nationalists.
I thought the Cossaks were gone too,
but they are back attacking Pussy Riot

on live TV. I understood my parents as paranoid,
and my daughter thinks the same of me.
Snowy landscape with a line of bare trees.
Pink sky at morning.

The Truth Is Mending

All those things you thought you could fix—
now you really wish your grandmother
was still alive to open her sewing box
and start you off with three feathers
on a Monday.
It would be like clockwork
without the winding key, and the mirrored
hands that reveal bruised shadows
beneath your eyes.
If the war were on
over here, drones would whistle
through the mountains like they do over there.
You would drop to the ground, whatever shape
your knees were in,
regardless of the full bag
of fruit and eggs you'd been lucky enough
to find in the market.
But that story belongs
with someone else's grandmother
over the ocean—your grandmother's wars
were also someplace else—
you marched against this war
and signed petitions; but lacked the strength
to rip the seams out of the demagogues'
uniforms. Instead,
you say the bruised Monday
has nothing at all to do with your landscape.

On The Way Out Of The Memory Palace

*I heard a definition once: Happiness is health and a short
memory!*   *—Audrey Hepburn*

Didn't Hannah Arendt write a book about forgetting,
or was that dozens of books written by Freud?
A mother claims, "I can't remember anything
from those years I was married to your father."
This covers the entire time the daughter lived at home,
plus a couple of years of college. The daughter's memory
is a cove, where unexpected fragments of a school play
wash up against a burnt tabletop. They have pills for that
nowadays, the mother tells her. The daughter remembers
the pink birth control pills the mother kept losing,
and the little helpers that drove the mother's huddled naps
on the couch after work. "Who can rest without
a little friendly assistance?" Now the mother is old
and must circumnavigate language, rewording all
the clichés. The daughter is addicted to crossword
puzzles with their little jolts of remembered trivia.

Repeat Emergencies Monitored

Some believe in lucid dreams:
enter the fields, pick poppies or asters,
and when the bear appears, instead
of running you engage the beast
in conversation, growing wise in the process.

Others believe in caffeine's ability
to lighten sleep, so when the door slams
you wake with a rapid heartbeat, the thump
of your pulse in your carotid artery, but nothing
else to report. Then there are sleeping pills,
so in the grogginess of morning all dissipates.

One proverb warns, "If you tell a dream
before breakfast, you'll be caught in the dream sea
all day." My daughter, the storyteller, is prone to that.
Controlling dreams seems a bit of a sham to me,
like recording every morsel of food in a diary,
keeping a ledger for official inspection.

Finding Myself Strange

By finding myself strange, what I mean is not
a form of psychosis, but that estrangement
where you walk through the world, and instead of *deja vu*
where everything has already occurred, events you know
have happened belong to someone else's life, even down
to wondering how that dishtowel with its landscape
of sea and compass appeared beside your sink,
which is you know is yours because it is in the kitchen
of the room next to the one with the bed you've arisen from.

If you are lucky this is related to travel, or if not
your ears are filled with the sound of your pulse
and the tintinnabulation of a song
you wouldn't have chosen to place on repeat.

Maybe you'd go to the sea; where the tidepools
would be waiting for you to pick through them
like the gatherers you descended from, living off
the corners of the fields, sleeping beside the lonely
stray dogs, playing a shepherd's pipe carved by a crazy
old man who had passed the age of his purple furies.
Each day the western sun would shock with the suddenness
of its descent though reds and oranges into blue twilight.

Like Happiness, And It Will Not Stand

Happiness refuses to stand still for
dissection—though really, what does?
Those rabbits were anesthetized
and tied down, so postdocs could watch
blood flow through the arteries of their hearts.
But return to ordinary happiness—Is it tied
to the heart, blind clench and release,
automatic until the end? Joy is episodic,
the way the first chocolate truffle far
exceeds the next. Chocolate and exercise
improve the heart. Does love lead to joy, or
its converse, laundry spilling onto the floor?
Those rabbits could care less about our hearts,
intact sacs of muscle beating patterns, life.

In the World Above

In the world above, Time closes
her book, puts away her pencil, says
"Let's have lunch," or "turn out the lights."
In the world below, seasons disappear
into geologic eras marked
by plumes of sulfurous gas.
When I lived beneath the sea,
water as blood, blood as salt,

I found friends in the low songs
of the whales, though even then
much was lost to my limited ears.
In the house above, I raise

the windows at night, and behind me
the husband closes them. I could
breathe the sea if they were open.
Instead we sit at the table,
and always someone says, "I'm cold,
I'm cold," or, "Pass the fish." I'm tempted
to answer in the language of the whales
but the air is so stingy with reverberation.

Prescription 1

In the light of the moon we identify
coordinates, only to see them wash
away in the orange sunrise. To find
the lost requires more than GPS
or map, compass and sextant.
In the shimmer of our peripheral
vision they are the same, reading
an old book, or baking brownies.
In a better world, we could take
the compass and a straight edge—
draw daisies, or enclose time
to hold everyone in a circle singing,
hands around one another's waists.

On Definitions

With all the ways time loops in the quantum
foam definitions slide away. Her mother
could have said "a life defined by sorrow"
but it might have been sparrows or tomorrow
which is a problem when tomorrow loops
around today. Her physics teacher would
have said "don't confuse your quantum world
with your mechanical space—no one
hoists anvils under an imaging machine."

Though isn't that the point: there is "no one"
on that infinitesimal scale so
we define life in the particle zoo:
>   Quarks—up and down bottom and strange
>   Leptons—neutrino, electron muon and tau

Imagine the first instants of the universe
where light and gravity interact
in long waves, when metaphors turn
upon themselves before they intersect
in hyperbolic geometries.

Gravity

Lends gravitas, however temporary
because if we were all in freefall, think
how childlike that would be;
careening into each other like new walkers,
holding onto the walls to avoid tottering,
drinking juice from boxes with straws;
but that is the least of it; sans gravity
we would lose the sanity of knowing
our bottoms from our tops; and we would reverse
other polarities, like true and false,
or in and out, until outboxes and inboxes
began to run together; time would lose
meaning, and the old and the young
would have a more equal relationship
to space. Eventually we would careen
out into the universe; small groups like seeds.

Nude Suite

i. Nude as Pronoun

Usually she, as it takes
a group for they.

When he is nude, action
follows: a cigarette
or a phone, or sports equipment.

They do not share the same frame.

ii. Nude As Metaphor

She wears her nakedness
the way another woman
would wear a corset.

His nude body softens
away from suited male
power.

iii. Nude as Conjunction

Connecting the dahlia
and the sea lion, or
the buried treasure
and the sand flies.

iv. Nude as Simile

Like water pumped
from the well;
like a door in that pause
between open and closed.

v. Nude as Personification

Of desire
because she is quite naked here,
stretched out on drapery;
that over-the-shoulder simile
implies reaction.

The Theory Headed Dragon

The left head snorts then inhales Marx
and exhales Lenin, while the right one
blasts Adam Smith into Ayn Rand.

>The inner music of desire
>Rock and Roll soundtrack
>fixed by 19.

The orator announces, "The lower organs
of the party must penetrate the backward
regions of the proletariat."

>Stravinsky declares printemps
>Broken rhythm denoting a complexity
>we played rotely in high school orchestra.

The theory headed dragon blasts between thickets
of hegemony, tail thrashing blaring televisions
through rose bushes that narrow the path.

>Horns blare insistent blues
>forcing submission
>from the marching band.

The dragon anoints itself with the glittering scales
of economists who win Nobel prizes for the elegant calculus
that proves we'd all be happier if the rich got richer.

>Pogoing to punk on the 8th floor
>and the music is never loud enough
>the party never large enough.

Moon rises on the Dragon's festival. Surplus armies
of the unemployed march arm in arm with
the fungible labor force, exchanging chants.

　　　The radio provides little comfort:
　　　On one frequency a gun-loving rant
　　　on the one above pimp-whore rap.

No one is neutral in the chamber
of the theory headed dragon. Each book shines
as elegant as a poem beaded by tiny footnotes.

　　　Imagine pattern: drifting into sleep
　　　at the Philip Glass concert,
　　　or to the insistent dance of blue grass.

At the end of the Dragon festival, trained handlers
clutching position papers direct the iridescent heads
to blow past each other powering

　　　A dirigible. It rises,
　　　painted in slogans that vanish
　　　into a one-hundred year silence.

This Is How the Wind Shifts

The wind shifts the way a cat knows how to trace
the path of a sparrow-hawk moth through fluctuating currents.

The wind shifts the way the stories in the news become
more and more detached from agreed upon facts.

The wind shifts into a storm complete with electrical
activity, and then hail deluges the street.

The wind shifts into the repeating electronic
delusions of reciprocal conversation.

The wind shifts so the teacher feels obliged to manufacture
optimism for the teens taking notes in the overcrowded room.

The wind shifts outside our imagination,
along with the cousin who emigrated to a far continent.

All That Remains

We listen for chords
      of the missing frogs
            that scudded along
                  this river.

Last night
      beside the water's edge
            pink traces of twilight
held the hour
      then vanished.

Carol Dorf is the author of *Every Evening Deserves A Title* (Delirious Nonce Publications.) Her poetry has been published in *Scientific American*, *The Journal of Humanistic Mathematics*, *Sin Fronteras*, *Antiphon*, *Spillway*, *OVS*, *Maintenant*, *The Mom Egg*, *Best Indie Lit New England*, and *Vinyl*. She is poetry editor of *Talking Writing* and teaches mathematics at Berkeley High School.

* 9 7 8 1 9 4 4 2 5 1 9 2 5 *